BEHIND
CLOSED
DOORS:

REAL MEN. REAL ISSUES.
REAL CONVERSATIONS. REAL SOLUTIONS.

REACHING & RENEWING MEN FOR THE KINGDOM! IT'S DAYTIME

MARQUIS L. COOPER

authorHOUSE

AuthorHouse™
1663 Liberty Drive
Bloomington, IN 47403
www.authorhouse.com
Phone: 833-262-8899

Published by AuthorHouse 10/12/2020

ISBN: 978-1-6655-0206-1 (sc)
ISBN: 978-1-6655-0205-4 (e)

Library of Congress Control Number: 2020918904

Print information available on the last page.

Any people depicted in stock imagery provided by Getty Images are models, and such images are being used for illustrative purposes only.
Certain stock imagery © Getty Images.

This book is printed on acid-free paper.

Scripture quotations marked NIV are taken from the Holy Bible, New International Version®. NIV®. Copyright © 1973, 1978, 1984 by International Bible Society. Used by permission of Zondervan. All rights reserved. [Biblica]

Scripture quotations marked MSG are taken from THE MESSAGE. Copyright © 1993, 1994, 1995, 1996, 2000, 2001, 2002, 2003 by Eugene H. Peterson. Used by permission of NavPress Publishing Group. Website.

CONTENTS

ACKNOWLEDGEMENTS

First and foremost, I want to thank God for giving me the vision to write this curriculum at such a time as this. I want to thank the greatest individuals in my life: my wife Karmen for always being in my corner pushing me to become the father, husband, and leader I have become. I want to thank my wonderful children: Marquis, Cobie, Nia, and Kalia. I want to thank all my family members who always believed in the gifts God had given me. I want to thank my lifelong friend Eric Norris for always being in my corner and supporting me for the past 40 years. I want to thank all my Otter Creek Community Church family for being the best church members on this side of heaven. All the members (men, women, children, and youth) at OCCC are God sent. I want to thank Donnell Parker (my father n law) who always reminded me to stay humble. I want to thank Shalada Toles and Latoya Davis for all the editorial work they put into this project. I want to thank a few of my adopted daughters: Mallory Gatson, Makayla Harris, Kristin Howard, Englysh Miller, and Courtnei Toney for always encouraging their "Father Coop" (this is the name they gave me as their high school counselor) to do more to help this generation of men. I want to thank my brother in Christ, Elder Corey Foreman for all the work he puts in to help our young men stay on the right side of the law, and for taking the time out of his busy schedule to write the Foreword. I want to thank all my former and present students for always encouraging me to keep moving forward. You guys really inspired me to keep making a difference in the lives of others. I am forever grateful to each of you. It is daytime!!!!

"I never thought I would be reading something so strong at such a young age. These are some of the most powerful questions I have ever seen in my life. These questions should make men want to be better. Mr. Cooper you are really going somewhere with this and I'm with you 100%"- **Jahari Irvin, Class of 2018, J.A. Fair High School of College and Career Academies**

This book is dedicated to the late Dr. William (Bill) Edwin Thomas- RIL Dr. Thomas aka "Doc"

FOREWORD

Rev. Marquis Cooper and I have shared many ministry moments helping men, young & old rise, just as the dry bones in the valley in the book of Ezekiel. Romans 8:30 reminds us that whom God predestinates, He also calls and whom he calls, He also justifies and whom He justifies, He also glorifies. I believe God called, predestined & justified Rev. Cooper and through Rev. Cooper's obedience to the call, God's glory is upon him.

Rev. Cooper is a nationally renowned motivational speaker, author, and professional school counselor. Most importantly, he is a carrier of the gospel. These great titles and acclamations are evidence that Rev. Cooper is exactly where he is supposed to be, doing the things that God has ordained him to do. I am proud to have witnessed the anointing in his life and to call him my friend.

Rev. Cooper and I share a passion for the mandate on our lives to spread the gospel. God has allowed us to be yoked together in the friendship for ministry. Marquis Cooper began his career as an educator after he graduated from Philander Smith College. But it was apparent that the call of God was upon his life as early as 4th grade. Since adolescence, he has been speaking to the masses and making a great impact in the lives of many. He has a God-given gift to meet people where they are and preach a relatable message of the power of faith and hope. He does this through discussing and attacking hidden issues that have become taboo in the church. One of the issues that he deals with so profoundly is sharing the history of the Willie Lynch letter to all cultures.

The Willie Lynch letter for many people including historians is a hoax primarily due to the language used in the letter. Many historians believe that some of the words used did not carry a connotation or meaning until almost 100 years later. Many critics simply believe that the letter has no merit based on the date that the letter was penned. Even with all the untruths that seem not credible, Marquis has been opening the eyes of people across the country since 2010 by expounding on two paragraphs which are imbedded in the Willie Lynch letter. These two paragraphs shed light on the decline of the black male and the growing concern of the black female in the 21st century.

Reverend Cooper and I believe that we will not be able to be who God has called us to be until the church begins to address specific topics. One of the biggest issues in the 21st century is strengthening and encouraging men to stay with God and their families. There continues to be a drastic decline of men in the 21st century church. Many churches across the nation have more women in attendance than that of men. Many of our sons will not understand the vital role of becoming the priest, provider, and protector of their homes unless we change this epidemic now.

If you have picked up this curriculum, then you have already answered the first call that God has extended to you. I believe your life is being changed now as you prepare to not just read this book, but to hear the voice of the Lord. Just as the dry bones heard the voice of the Lord, I declare that you can hear the voice of the Lord and live again. The Lord stands at the door of your heart; will you let Him in? It is Rev. Cooper's desire that you will live and declare the works of the Lord and live to the highest extent of your purpose.

Rev. Cooper and I agree that purpose is being unveiled and manifestations of God's word are being revealed in your life and heart. Rev. Cooper serves as a model of the word that he preaches. Allow him to help navigate you to a place of healing as he discusses various issues from a place of honesty.

Blessings be upon you Rev. Cooper for having an ear to hear from God and being obedient to the Holy Spirit to help us. God bless you my brother! Blessings be upon the reader for being obedient to the call to read this book and being ignited to be a better child of God, and a better man for the Kingdom.

Corey Foreman

INTRODUCTION

How to save our men has been a topic of discussion that has taken place in schools, churches, community centers, and other venues across this country for years. As a pastor, father, school counselor, and community leader, I understand the many challenges that our males are faced with each day. I also believe there is a solution to a problem that seems to be out of control. I was born and raised in a small town in Eastern Arkansas called Marianna, Arkansas. I am the youngest of 22 children in my family, and family has always been a top priority for me.

Marianna was a city to be proud of, primarily due to the notable individuals who are from Marianna. Individuals such as Charlie Flowers, Carlos Hall, Oliver Lake, Robert McFerrin, Oscar Polk, Jean Yarbrough, and Rodney Slater who served as the United States Secretary of Transportation from 1997 to 2001. During the late 80's the image of the town slowly began to fall apart, and this created a dark shadow that the city has never been able to fully recover from. Some people believed that if you were from Marianna, then your fate was sealed. Marianna only produced thugs, murderers, criminals, or drug dealers. Part of the reason for writing this curriculum is to REACH and RENEW our men before they become part of a vicious cycle.

At some point in history, a seed of irresponsibility grew in our males. As a result, the prison system is overpopulated, and we have done little to change the outcome. I believe there is something we can do to reclaim our males, and it starts with shifting the male into his proper position in the household.

Please allow me to paint a picture and make it clear. The standard order for a two-parent household is that of the father, wife, son, and daughter. A plan was devised many years ago that changed the structure of the family, especially the positioning of the male. This plan was written by Willie Lynch in 1712. In this book, he basically describes a perfect plan to keep the African American culture from ever attaining life to the fullest. What Lynch did not account for, was a rise in single parent homes regardless of ethnicity. What was once only written for African Americans now mirrors the homes of many ethnic groups across this country. In many homes the family structure looks like the following: You have the son (in an unknown spot), mother (in the father's spot), daughter (behind her mother out of her spot), and the father (totally removed from the family; he has no spot). Here is an illustration for those of you who are visual learners; please read from left to right.

Normal Family Structure	Father (head of house)	Wife (beside the head)	Son (beside the mother)	Daughter (beside the brother)
Dysfunctional Family Structure	Wife (positioned where the father was)	Daughter (positioned behind her mom)	Father (positioned nowhere)	Son (positioned beside his mom on left side)

When this style of familial transfer takes place, it has a profound effect on the entire family unit, but mostly with the male. The good news is there is still hope to change the fate of many males regardless of ethnicity. We can no longer allow our males to fail in life because they have no support team in place. I truly believe that many of our males are dropping out of high schools, becoming teenaged fathers, going to prison, selling drugs, being captivated by the entertainment world, and not living up to their God given potential because they simply don't have the role models to help them become successful in life. We can no longer make excuses for not reaching back to save our men; both the young and old.

The plight of men regardless of ethnicity seems to be getting worse by the minute. A lot of young males have no idea of what it takes to be a good leader because they have never seen one. Therefore, the writing of this manual is so timely because I believe if people whole heartedly believe there is no hope for the youth, then we as a nation will be doomed. However, there is hope to save this generation of young males, but it all starts with knowing, believing, and internalizing that things can get better.

Through the power of being real and transparent, we can save the lives of countless males of all ethnic groups in this generation. This curriculum will start us on the journey to help shift this vicious cycle in our country. The time for us to RENEW & REACH men in this country is NOW!!! It is Daytime!!!

SUGGESTIONS FOR USING THIS MANUAL

I. *HELPFUL MATERIALS*
1. Internet access (for you to research information that you may need clarity on).
2. Your Bible (read the Message version) to look up unfamiliar scriptures.
3. Use a pencil. Do not use ink because you may change your answers.
4. A journal or notebook to jot down other thoughts you may have as you read.

II. *HINTS FOR PERSONAL STUDY*
1. Remove all distractions as you prepare to begin a journey for change.
2. Answer each question as thorough as you can.
3. Feel free to highlight things that stand out to you as you read.
4. Read each question until the question becomes a part of you.

III. *HOW TO GET THE MOST OUT OF YOUR CLASS TIME*
1. Attend every class.
2. Answer the questions in the workbook PRIOR to attending your class.
3. Have follow up questions already written down in your personal notebook.

IV. *HOW THIS STUDY IS LAID OUT*
1. The study consists of 7 lessons if being done in a group the study can be repeated every quarter as men join.
2. The lessons build on one another, so it is important to work through all the material in the order that it is laid out.
3. Each lesson includes Scripture that should be studied and discussion questions that help you integrate the material into your own life.
4. Be honest and truthful with yourself as you answer the questions.
5. This study is not designed to be done alone (participate in a small group if available). If no group is available, find an accountability partner to work with.
6. Share your experience of growth with others as you complete this journey (do not keep this information all to yourself

GETTING TO KNOW YOU

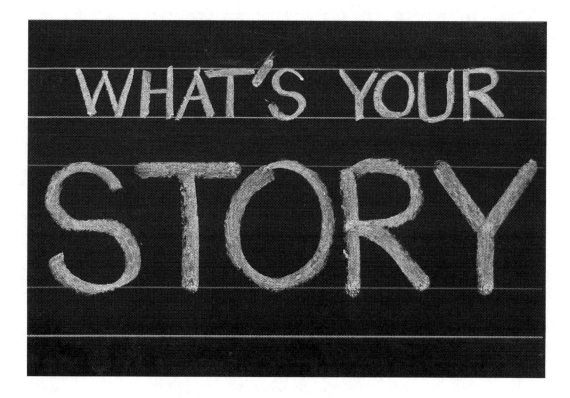

PLEASE ANSWER THESE QUESTIONS HONESTLY

My greatest struggle is (**a struggle is defined as something you want to change about yourself, but you just don't know how**)

_____

_____

_____

_____

_____

If there was one thing I could change about myself it would be the way I....

_____

_____

_____

_____

_____

_____

What is one question you always wanted to ask someone while growing up, but never had the courage to ask?

_____

_____

_____

_____

_____

_____

Do you have a relationship with Christ? Have you ever been baptized? Do you remember the minister who baptized you?

_____

_____

_____

_____

_____

_____

Do you understand what salvation or being saved is all about? What does this mean to you?

_____

_____

_____

_____

_____

_____

Do you remember how old you were when you accepted Christ into your life? What was that process like for you? Did you fully understand what you were doing?

_____

_____

_____

_____

_____

_____

Now that you have completed these preliminary questions get ready to take a journey which will help you become a true disciple of Christ. This is a journey which will help you RENEW yourself and REACH other men.

LESSON 1

REAL TALK 101

I was born and raised in a small town in Eastern Arkansas called Marianna, Arkansas. Marianna's population sits under 4,000 people. Being the youngest of 22 children in my family was always a plus for me. When I was younger, I often took advantage of my older siblings who were doing well in life. During the summer months I was always vacationing, shopping, and enjoying the life of being the youngest of the family. I was fortunate to grow up with both parents in the home. My parents were married for over 30 years before we lost my dad in 2006. I can honestly say I had my fair share of both positive and negative situations while growing up, but I used every known opportunity to learn from them both. One of the many things life has taught me is the ability to make conscious decisions which can either negatively or positively impact and hinder your purpose in life. I have men in my family who unfortunately made decisions which landed them in prison and some who even died from gun violence. I recently lost a nephew to gun violence. He was an aspiring rap artist whose life abruptly ended way too soon. One of the things I try to impress upon my son is that he doesn't have to become a statistic if he learns from the past mistakes of others. We have way too many men who are becoming statistics in this country. Some are born into situations which push them towards this path, and some willingly choose this path because they refuse to listen. This chapter will shed light on many issues that probably never crossed your mind.

STATISTICS ABOUT MEN IN THE 21ST CENTURY

57.6 % of black children, 31.2% of Hispanic children, and 20.7% of white children are living without their father being present in the home.

What factors do you believe led to such a drastic increase of fathers leaving the home or never being present in the home?

_____

_____

_____

_____

_____

The average father gives only 35 seconds of undivided attention to his child each day. Why do you think this is the case? Do you agree or disagree with this statement?

_____

_____

_____

_____

_____

According to U.S. Census Bureau an estimated 19.7 million children live without their father. Why do women continue to have children by men who have no desire to father their child?

_____

_____

_____

_____

_____

Statics show 73% males between the ages of 18-35 are either in prison, on probation, or on parole. Why do you think this number is so high?

_____

_____

_____

_____

_____

_____

Homicide and Suicide is the leading cause of death for black males between the ages of 13-25. Do you think the church is doing enough to address this issue as it relates to black males?

_____

_____

_____

_____

_____

_____

Do you think labeling boys as being "bad" when they are young influences them not coming to church when they get older?

_____

_____

_____

_____

_____

_____

Black males account for 13.7 percent of suspensions each year in school. Hispanics account for 4.5 percent, whites account for 3.4 percent, and Asians account for1.1 percent of all suspensions.

Why do you think these numbers are so drastically different? Do you think the lack of the father not being present in the home is the vast difference in these figures? Why or why not?

_____

_____

_____

_____

_____

By 2030, it is projected that one out of every three prisoners will be over 50 years old. What can men in the church do to change this outcome?

_____

_____

_____

_____

_____

HOW MANY PEOPLE TODAY CAN EXCLAIM WITH DIGNITY WHAT PETER SAYS IN ACTS 3:4?

Acts 3:4 reads, *Peter with John at his side, looked him straight in the eye and said, "Look here." He looked up, expecting to get something from them.*

What was the importance of Peter saying, "Look here"? What did the man think he was going to receive from them when he looked up?

_____

_____

_____

_____

_____

How do we help men become independent without always giving them money? Do you think money is the answer to solve all problems?

_____

_____

_____

_____

_____

How do men reclaim their position and status in the family with the stats being as they currently are?

_____

_____

_____

_____

_____

What are five things men can do to attack issues such as: absent fathers, high death rates, incarceration, high school dropout rates….

1. _____

2. _____

3. _____

4. _____

5. _____

HISTORICAL CONTRIBUTING FACTORS LEADING TO THE MORAL DECLINE AMONG BLACK MEN DURING THE SLAVERY ERA

Black couples could not marry.
Black couples were forbidden to live under the same roof.
Black couples lived in nuclear families.
Black men were often sold and separated from their families.

How did families being separated during slavery destroy the black family structure?

_____

_____

_____

_____

_____

ADAM, WHERE ARE YOU?

Genesis 3:9 reads, *God called to the Man: "Where are you?"* Why does God come in the garden looking for Adam and not Eve?

_____

_____

_____

_____

_____

Seven questions we need to be asking the present-day Adam **(all these questions may not apply to you but answer truthfully in your heart if they do).**

1. Adam, you say you have come out of slavery but where are you now economically?
2. Adam, why are so many women void of your male presence in the home forcing her to seek public assistance?
3. Adam, you say you can stand on your own two feet, so why are you still depending upon a woman to take care of you?
4. Adam, you say you care about the country, but when was the last time you voted?
5. Adam, where are you intellectually? What are you doing to enhance your intellectual growth monthly?
6. Adam, when was the last time you read a book in its entirety? What book did you read?
7. Adam, when was the last time you led your family in prayer and an in-depth study of God's awesome word?

How many of these seven questions hit home? Was there one where you really felt convicted?

_____

_____

_____

_____

_____

Which one of the seven questions frustrates you the most with this generation of men?

_____

_____

_____

_____

_____

Which question did you ponder the most?

_____

_____

_____

_____

_____

What are three things men can do to help address these issues?

_____

_____

_____

_____

_____

What struck you the most as you were reading the information in this lesson?

_____

_____

_____

_____

_____

After answering these questions in Lesson 1, do you have a better idea of the problems, we are now faced with in the 21st century? Did you know we were faced with all these issues before reading Chapter 1? What is your immediate personal plan of action to help combat these issues?

_____

_____

_____

_____

_____

_____

_____

Who is the most positive role model in your life at this moment? What makes this individual stand out to you? After you write about this individual, please let them know.

_____

_____

_____

_____

_____

_____

_____

LESSON 1

REAL TALK 101

Cooper's Nuggets 4 the week

- ❖ Speaking idle words will create destruction in our lives. What is spoken can impact us both negatively and positively. Your words form your world!
- ❖ Proverbs 18:21 (MSG) - *Words kill, words give life: they're either poison or fruit- you choose.*
- ❖ It's time to clean your "house" (state of mind). What happens in your house no longer must stay in your house. YOU CAN RELEASE IT STARTING TODAY!!!
- ❖ What you don't know won't simply hurt you; it can KILL you!

Question to Consider

What are three things you learned from Lesson 1 that you are willing to share with other men?

- ❖ 1. _____
- ❖ 2. _____
- ❖ 3. _____

<u>Point to Ponder</u>

"When people try to kill your gift by keeping you SILENT, find another way to speak without TALKING. Your gift can SPEAK without you saying one WORD"- Marquis L. Cooper

NOTES

LESSON 2

REAL MEN. REAL PROVIDERS.

As a young child I was aware there was a God. I was also aware God had given me a spiritual gift at an early age in life. While growing up there were times when my parents did not go to church on Sunday, but they would always ensure I made it to church anytime the doors were open. As I began to mature in Christ, I began to become more active in church which eventually led to me becoming a Junior Sunday School Superintendent at the age of 14. It was at this time I learned how to pray and speak to God, how to fellowship with other Christians, and truly gained an understanding of the role of the family from a biblical standpoint. I learned at an early age there is divine order in family. The bible teaches us four simple truths which are: 1). Children honor your parents, 2). Fathers do not provoke your children to anger, 3). Husbands love your wives and 4). Wives respect and support the leadership of your husbands. These four truths I learned as a child carried over into my adult years. I Corinthians 13:11 reads, *"When I was a child, I talked like a child, I thought like a child, I reasoned like a child, but when I became a man, I put the ways of childhood behind me"*. For some odd reason we still have way too many men who have never allowed this scripture to resonate in their spirits. My father always provided for the needs of his family even at times when it was a struggle for him. My father did not graduate from high school, but always instilled in his children we needed to go as far as we could in life educationally. These life lessons are the lessons I now instill into my own children.

LESSON 2

REAL MEN. REAL PROVIDERS.

The three biblical characteristics of being a man are to be a priest, provider, and protector.

The first biblical characteristic of manhood is being a **priest.** When you were growing up were you taught that being a priest, provider, or protector was important? If not, what were you taught? Do you still see things the same way now that you are older?

_____

_____

_____

_____

_____

_____

A priest is defined as one who brings the people to God. When you were growing up, who do you remember teaching you about God (if this was taught in your home)? What did they teach you that still stands out?

_____

_____

_____

_____

_____

It is the spiritual duty of the man to be "the priest of his family". Why do we have more women trying to be the priest in the 21st century? Is this okay? Why is this happening?

_____

_____

_____

_____

_____

Where did we start to see a decline as it relates to men being priest over their households? What caused this decline? You can search the internet or just answer this question based on your personal perception?

_____

_____

_____

_____

_____

_____

The man should always pray, meditate in the word, fellowship with believers, and be witnessing on behalf of the kingdom. Why do you think the man has stopped many of the above practices?

_____

_____

_____

_____

_____

_____

The second biblical responsibility of the man is to be a **provider** for his family. What does a provider look like to you?

_____

_____

_____

_____

_____

_____

A true father takes his responsibility to his family seriously and honors his role as a provider. Why has this role drastically declined?

_____

_____

_____

_____

_____

A pauper is defined as an extremely poor person, and a provider is who one brings something to the table. The provider is known as the "bread winner".

How do we transform men from being a "pauper" to being a dignified "provider"? What are some things that can be put in place to change this scenario?

_____

_____

_____

_____

_____

When you were growing up, who was the "bread winner" in your house?

_____

_____

_____

The third biblical responsibility is to be a **protector** of his family. What does it mean to be a protector?

_____

_____

_____

_____

A man cannot sufficiently serve as a "protector" of his family when he is not right with God. What does it mean to be "right with God"?

_____

_____

_____

_____

Read II Samuel 13:1-21 (Message bible)

What did you learn from reading this story? What kind of friend was Jonadab? How would you have felt if Tamar were your sister? Why did Amnon hate her after he raped her? Why did Absalom tell her to forget about what he did in verse 20? If you had been the king what would you have done? What lessons did you take away from reading this passage of scripture?

_____

_____

_____

_____

_____

_____

_____

_____

What are some additional questions you can ask other men to expound on from reading II Samuel 13:1-21?

_____

_____

_____

_____

What does being a responsible man in the 21st century look like? What does being an irresponsible man look like?

_____

_____

_____

_____

Name five men you look up to. Why are these men so influential in your life? What makes them stand out?

_____

_____

_____

_____

_____

~⌘~

LESSON 2

REAL MEN. REAL PROVIDERS.

Cooper's Nuggets for the week

- ❖ The circle of change begins with knowing who you really are.
- ❖ We all need support from others. Don't ever be too prideful to ask for help.
- ❖ It's time for men to take back their rightful positions in life.

Question to Consider

- ❖ A man's strength is in his character. Character is defined as the mental and moral qualities distinctive to an individual. Does your character reflect who you really are? Why or why not?

_____

_____

_____

❖ What are three things you learned from Lesson 2 that you are willing to share with other men?

❖ 1. _____

❖ 2. _____

❖ 3. _____

Point to Ponder

❖ **When you are really trying to grow, you must move beyond those who have stopped growing. It is OKAY- Marquis Cooper**

NOTES

REAL ISSUES

One of the biggest problems many men deal with is how to forgive those who hurt them, hypocrisy, how to empower each other, and the spirit of traditionalism. Matthew 5:44 reads, *"But I tell you, love your enemies and pray for those who persecute you"*. This is a very tough scripture for men to grasp their minds around because it's very hard to love those who you know don't mean you any good, yet the bible teaches us to not only love them, but also to pray for them. In my life I've had to forgive people who purposely set out to destroy my ministry because of envy, jealously, and strife. It was in those very moments where God was teaching me not to look at the person who was attacking me, but to focus on the spirit where the attack was coming from. Men I can assure you that this type of spiritual growth can only be attained with tons of prayer and a mindset to want to see things differently. As men, we are constantly being attacked by other men, and we quickly forget "hurt people, hurt people". There are a lot of hurt and broken men in this world, but society has taught us not to show any signs of being broken. This often leads to men not being able to reconcile with their fellow brethren, and not being able to get the proper counseling needed to cope with life issues. The book of 2 Corinthians 5:18 reads, *"All this is from God, who reconciled us to himself through Christ and gave us the ministry of reconciliation"*. The entire message of reconciliation is centered around the love of God and the death of Christ. This lesson will deal with each of these areas in their respective ways. Be open and honest as you answer each of these questions. John 8:32- *"And you will know the truth, and the truth will set you free"*. It is Daytime!!!!

As you analyze your life today, what are the top five issues facing you in life right now? Place them in order from least to greatest?

_____

_____

_____

_____

_____

Zig Ziglar is quoted as saying "everybody needs recognition". How are most men in the 21st century recognized?

_____

_____

_____

_____

_____

Philippians 3:17 (MSG) states, *"Stick with me friends. Keep track of those you see running this same course, headed for the same goal"*. What does this scripture teach you?

_____

_____

_____

_____

_____

We must see our brothers as God sees them. God does not remind our brothers of their past sins, but points them toward a brighter future.

Why do we have such a hard time forgiving people when they hurt us? Have you ever hurt someone? If so, did you want them to forgive you for what you did to them?

_____

_____

_____

_____

_____

Why is forgiveness such a big problem amongst believers?

_____

_____

_____

_____

_____

What does the phrase "hurt people, hurt people" mean?

_____

_____

_____

_____

_____

Authentic ministry can take place in the lives of men if we are willing to cancel traditions of the past that bind (tie down) rather than liberate (free) us. What does this statement mean to you?

_____

_____

_____

_____

_____

_____

Matthew 15:6-9 (MSG) reads, "These people make a big show of saying the right thing, but their heart isn't in it. They act like they are worshipping me, but they do not mean it. They just use me as a cover for teaching whatever suits their fancy." What does this scripture mean to you?

_____

_____

_____

_____

_____

_____

What did you get from reading this? Do you feel many people in the church act like this now? Do you see yourself in this scripture? If so how?

_____

_____

_____

_____

_____

_____

What does *"they just use me as a cover for teaching whatever suits their fancy"* mean to you?

_____

_____

_____

_____

_____

Ezekiel 37:1-4 (MSG) reads, "God grabbed me. God's Spirit took me up and set me down in the middle of an open plain strewn with bones. He led me around and among them- a lot of bones! There were bones all over the plain-dry bones, bleached by the sun. He said to me, "Son of man, can these bones live?" I said, "Master God, only you know that." He said to me, "Prophesy over these bones: 'Dry bones, listen to the Message of God!"

What did you learn from reading these verses? Does this resemble how America looks now? What can you do as a man to help people who are not living in their purpose? Why did God put it back on Ezekiel to speak life into the dry bones?

_____

_____

_____

_____

_____

Psalms 107:1-3(MSG) reads, Oh, thank God- he is so good! His love never runs out. All of you set free by God, tell the world! Tell how he freed you from oppression, then rounded you up from all over the place, from the four winds, from the seven seas.

What do these scriptures teach you about God? Is this how you view God?

_____

_____

_____

_____

_____

Job 14:14 (MSG) reads, *"We're all adrift in the same boat: too few days, too many troubles.* Do you feel the same way Job feels in this scripture? Have you experienced more good days or more bad days in your life? How did you overcome the trials of life?

_____

_____

_____

_____

_____

_____

Psalms 34:6 (MSG) reads, *"When I was desperate, I called out, and God got me out of a tight spot".* How many times have you found yourself in a tight spot in life? What did you promise God you would do differently if God got you out? Did you keep or break your promise to God?

_____

_____

_____

_____

_____

_____

John Chapter 11 deals with the story of a man named Lazarus. Lazarus had been dead for a total of four days, but Jesus raised him from the dead. Why was it important for Jesus to raise Lazarus from the grave? Has God ever delivered you from a dead issue in your life? If so, what was the issue?

_____

_____

_____

_____

_____

_____

What can we do to wake up our "dead" men?

_____

_____

_____

_____

_____

Luke 7:11-15 (MSG) reads, "Not long after that, Jesus went to the village Nain. His disciples were with him, along with quite a large crowd. As they approached the village gate, they met a funeral procession- a woman's only son was being carried out for burial. And the mother was a widow. When Jesus saw her, his heart broke. He said to her "Don't cry." Then he went over and touched the coffin. The pallbearers stopped. He said, "Young man, I tell you: Get up." The dead son sat up and began talking. Jesus presented him to his mother.

What did you learn about the heart of Jesus from reading this story? Why did Jesus have compassion for this woman? Has Jesus ever shown up in your life when it looked like everything was over? What is your biggest take away from reading this story?

_____

_____

_____

_____

_____

What can men in the church do to help ensure that men in the community reach their highest potential in life?

_____

_____

_____

_____

_____

_____

REAL ISSUES

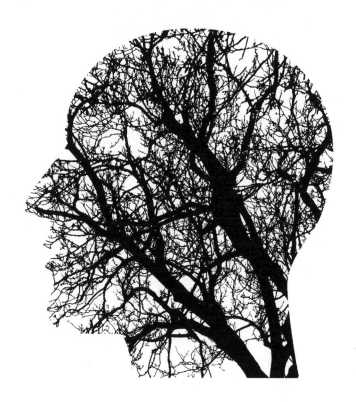

Cooper's Nuggets for the week

- ❖ All men have issues!!!
- ❖ You must be open and honest about where you are in life.
- ❖ Everyone who knows you needs you to become YOU!!!

Question to Consider

- ❖ What is one mistake you truly regret you made in life?

_____

_____

_____

❖ What are three things you learned from Lesson 3 that you are willing to share with other men?

❖ 1. _____

❖ 2. _____

❖ 3. _____

Point to Ponder

❖ "Stay away from people who say that other people got what they deserved. The truth of the matter is we all deserve something, and we need to pray every day that we don't get what we all rightfully deserve"- Marquis Cooper

NOTES

REAL CONVERSATIONS

Sometimes in life one of the greatest things one can do for himself is to truly be reflective. Doing so helps you to grow and learn. One of the greatest accounts of this truth can be found in the life of David. The bible calls David a man after God's own heart (Acts 13:22). Yet, as you may or may not know, David committed some sins that most people probably would not be so quick to forgive, even if someone forgave them. The story of David and Bathsheba reminds us that even men who were considered to be great in the sight of God still struggled with overcoming fleshly matters in their lives. David made many mistakes in 2 Samuel Chapter 11 (please stop and read this entire chapter before continuing). I can imagine that most of you were blown away as you read the accounts of Chapter 11. David's lustful desire for Bathsheba led him to execute six sins that God would forgive, but David still had to reap the consequences of his actions.

2 Samuel 12: 13-14 reads, *"Then David said to Nathan, "I have sinned against the Lord." Nathan replied, "The Lord has taken your sin. You are not going to die. 14- But because by doing this you have*

shown utter contempt for the Lord, the son born to you will die.” This was a hard pill to swallow for David, but we must remember that even though God is a merciful and just God, He cannot allow his children to sin willingly without a consequence. David's consequence would be his son would die on the seventh day he was born (2 Samuel 12:18). As you read these accounts about David, you still may be wondering why God called David, “a man after his own heart.” David had three traits that led Him to echo these words about the heart of David. David was obedient, dependent, and repentant. It is my desire that God will call each of us “a man after His own heart”.

ANSWER THESE QUESTIONS AGAIN (THE FIRST THREE QUESTIONS) TO SEE IF YOUR RESPONSE HAS CHANGED FROM WHEN YOU ANSWERED THEM IN LESSON 1

My greatest struggle is (**a struggle is defined as something you want to change about yourself, but you just don't know how**)

_____

_____

_____

_____

_____

If there was one thing, I could change about myself it would be the way I ….

_____

_____

_____

_____

What is one question you have always wanted to ask, but never had the courage to?

_____

_____

_____

_____

What does this quote mean to you, "When the man is out of place, the woman becomes displaced, and the children become misplaced"?

_____

_____

_____

_____

_____

What has happened to the order of the family in the 21st century?

_____

_____

_____

_____

_____

Why do many people say men are hopeless? Do you agree or disagree with this statement?

_____

_____

_____

_____

_____

What is the biggest problem you've encountered in the past when dealing with women (BE HONEST)?

_____

_____

_____

_____

_____

In most churches in America women outnumber men four to one. Why do you think this number is so high? Do you think men even realize the disparity (great difference) in the church?

_____

_____

_____

_____

_____

Some men say the church and other spiritual leaders participate in the verbal demeaning of the man. Do you agree or disagree with this statement? Why or why not?

_____

_____

_____

_____

_____

_____

According to some men, women spend more time at church than at home. Should women cater to the church more than they cater to their husbands? What problem does this create in the eyes of men? Should men be competing with the church? What can we do to solve this issue?

_____

_____

_____

_____

_____

_____

_____

What is the difference between Mother's Day and Father's Day?

_____

_____

_____

_____

_____

Do we promote each holiday the same way in the church? Why do you think there's such a big difference between the two? Do you think men are bothered by this? Why or why not?

_____

_____

_____

_____

_____

_____

What major issues are some young men dealing with in the 21st century? Are these issues getting more out of control? Do you feel there is any hope to reverse some of these issues?

_____

_____

_____

_____

_____

_____

What has caused the 21ˢᵗ century family to become so frail (weak and delicate)?

_____

_____

_____

_____

_____

How can we begin to address the issues that are taking place in our communities?

_____

_____

_____

_____

_____

_____

Can you remember the strong families in your communities when you were growing up? What made them stand apart from other families?

_____

_____

_____

_____

_____

_____

_____

_____

LESSON 4

REAL CONVERSATIONS

Cooper's Nuggets for the week

- ❖ The only way to truly deal with life is to be honest with self.
- ❖ Hurt people, hurt people!!
- ❖ Sometimes in life you must remove yourself (get rid of distractions) so you can see yourself.
- ❖ "When your present is not in order, your future is in danger of being chaotic"- Marquis Cooper

Question to Consider

- ❖ Are you willing to take responsibility for every area in your life that needs improvement?

❖ What are three things you learned from Lesson 4 that you are willing to share with other men?

❖ 1. _____

❖ 2. _____

❖ 3. _____

Point to Ponder

❖ "When you get tired of doing the SAME THING you will get serious about doing SOMETHING ELSE. It's not enough to SEE what you want; you have to start MOVING towards what you WANT"- Marquis Cooper

NOTES

LESSON 5

REAL MEN ARE LEGIT

On September 5,1991 M.C. Hammer released a song called "2 Legit 2 Quit". This song proved to be successful in the U.S., peaking at the Top 10 of the Billboard Hot 100. The meaning of the word in 1991 had a simple implication which was this, keep the momentum flowing no matter what. This is what led to this song being so popular to all who listened to it. I can still remember being in the hallway changing classes and someone would yell out "2 Legit, 2 Legit 2 Quit". Everyone would start chanting the words and people would start dancing all the way to class. As you can probably tell M.C. Hammer got us into a lot of trouble in the 90's. The beat, the energy, and the words of the song literally propelled you to bring more to the table each day. Over the past 30 years, being a father, role model, and mentor has drastically lost all its meaning. We are now facing unprecedented times where there is such a disconnect with men being fathers and leaders, that the time has arrived where the word LEGIT must take on a new meaning. **L.E.G.I.T.** is an acronym which stands for **Loyal, Edifying, God Fearing, Integrity filled, and Transparent.** My prayer is that this acronym will become imbedded into the hearts and mind of every man who goes through this curriculum. God is calling all of us to a higher standard and it is my prayer all of us will answer the call. As you read this chapter keep the acronym LEGIT at the forefront of your thought process and challenge other men to do the same. The time is NOW!!!!

What does LEGIT mean to you?

_____

_____

_____

_____

_____

How many of those five traits from the previous page do you presently possess? Which ones do you struggle with the most?

_____

_____

_____

_____

_____

What trait (s) from the previous page do you personally feel men in the church are struggling with? The traits are Loyal, Edifying, God Fearing, Integrity filled, and Transparent.

_____

_____

_____

_____

_____

Do you think having integrity is important? Why or why not?

_____

_____

_____

_____

_____

Integrity preserves continuity. This means being the same person in private as you are in public. Is this the case for most men? Is this the case for you? Why or why not?

_____

_____

_____

_____

_____

_____

Read Proverbs 18:24, Matthew 7:12, and Galatians 6:7

Proverbs 18:24 (MSG) reads, _"Friends come, and friends go, but a true friend sticks by you like family"_. How many true friends would you say you have? Would you consider yourself to be a friend? Why do you think you fit this category?

_____

_____

_____

_____

_____

_____

Matthew 7:12 (MSG) reads, *"Here is a simple, rule-of-thumb guide for behavior: Ask yourself what you want people to do for you, then grab the initiative and do it for them"*. What does this scripture mean to you?

_____

_____

_____

_____

_____

_____

Galatians 6:7-8 (MSG) reads, *"Don't be misled: No one makes a fool of God. What a person plants, he will harvest. The person who plants selfishness, ignoring the needs of others-ignoring God! —harvests a crop of weeds. All he will have to show for his life is weeds! But the one who plants in response to God, letting God's Spirit do the growth work in him, harvests a crop of real life, eternal life.*

What does this scripture teach you? How do you see yourself in this scripture? Have you ever felt like you were making a fool out of God?

_____

_____

_____

_____

_____

Men lacking integrity have issues with being examples of truth. What does this mean to you?

_____

_____

_____

_____

_____

The Christian church normally suffers because of leaders who lack integrity.

What recent issues have shaken the foundation of the church?

_____

_____

_____

_____

_____

_____

What has happened to the integrity factor in this country? What happened to the integrity factor in the church?

_____

_____

_____

_____

_____

_____

Loyalty is defined as being faithful to a person, an idea, a custom, a cause, or a duty. What are some things in the 21st century that are causing men not to be loyal?

_____

_____

_____

_____

_____

_____

What does loyalty mean to you?

_____

_____

_____

_____

_____

Who is the most loyal man you know/knew? What makes him this way?

_____

_____

_____

_____

_____

Once a man compromises with sin, his credibility is damaged. Why is credibility important as it relates to being children of God?

_____

_____

_____

_____

_____

Not being loyal to God will make you ineffective in your homes, the workplace, and places of society. Why is this case?

_____

_____

_____

_____

_____

John 13:23 (MSG) reads, *"One of the disciples, the one Jesus loved dearly, was reclining against him, his head on his shoulder"*. Why do you think Jesus referred to John this way? Do you think he loved the other disciples? What was it about John that made him stand out to Jesus?

_____

_____

_____

_____

_____

How can we to create this type of harmony among men in our society? Jesus displayed that men should be able lean on each other. How can we get men to learn how to trust each other?

_____

_____

_____

_____

_____

LESSON 5

REAL MEN ARE LEGIT

Cooper's Nuggets for the week

- ❖ The truth will set you free, but first it may hurt you.
- ❖ Without integrity you really have nothing.
- ❖ Every man needs to have at least one loyal brother in his corner.
- ❖ God will never leave you nor forsake you.

Question to Consider

❖ In what area of your life are you lacking loyalty?

_____

_____

_____

❖ What are three things you learned from Lesson 5 that you are willing to share with other men?

❖ 1. _____

❖ 2. _____

❖ 3. _____

Point to Ponder

❖ "Some people are waiting on you to ARRIVE so they can START. Your DESTINATION is their BEGINNING"- Marquis Cooper

NOTES

LESSON 6

R.A.C.P. MEN

"I was responsible while waiting on you. I was accountable in my search to find you.
I was consistent while I was looking for you. I have to be persistent so that I become
the man God designed me to be so that I don't lose you"-Marquis Cooper

God dropped this quote in my spirit 12 years ago, and since that moment things have never been the same. This quote changed my total outlook on what I needed to teach my daughter and other young ladies as it related to what they needed to look for in a man when they started dating. It also changed my perspective as to what I needed to teach my son and other males on what their approach should be when they start dating. Men and women are raised in two totally different ways in America. Men are taught to be the providers for their families. The problem with this is that most men only equate this to working and providing the income necessary to take care of their families. Women, on the other hand, are taught to be faithful in their relationships, to always keep the house in order, to take good care of the child(ren), and to keep God at the forefront of their lives. This list does not seem quite fair when you compare them side by side. These lists being different are the primary reason for me sharing this pertinent information in this chapter. Girls were taught the importance of family early in life because many grew up playing make believe family with their dolls, cooking in their toy kitchens, and having sleepovers with their best friends. Boys on the other hand spent most of their time playing video games, playing sports, and learning how to take care of things on the outside of the house. This chapter is dedicated solely to helping men discover their potential in becoming a R.A.C.P. man in the 21st century, because our daughters and women deserve only the best from all of us.

Why is it important for men to teach their sons how to become R.A.C.P. men? R.A.C.P. men are those who will always be RESPONSIBLE for their actions, ACCOUNTABLE to the people they love, CONSISTENT in finishing what they start, and PERSISTENT in achieving their God given vision in life.

_____

_____

_____

_____

_____

_____

Do you think most women know what to look when dating a man? If you have a daughter will you teach her to look for the above traits when she starts dating? Why or why not?

_____

_____

_____

_____

_____

_____

When you were growing up how did most men tell you to live? Did their words help you or hinder you? This is perhaps why we have so many misguided men (young) in this world because there wasn't a strong well versed man/men in his life to guide him from wrong doings so he had to endure unnecessary hardships in life and learn from those mistakes. What will you do to ensure this next generation does not experience what you experienced growing up?

_____

_____

_____

_____

_____

When you were growing up did you struggle or was everything just given to you? Do you think struggling early makes you better prepared for life later?

_____

_____

_____

_____

_____

Do you think it is important for a man to teach his children how to persevere when life does not go as planned?

_____

_____

_____

_____

_____

Is it easy for men to give up on God when they are going through a crisis? Do you turn to God first or do you turn to others first when you hit a crisis in life?

_____

_____

_____

_____

_____

The greatest example of a man who endured a crisis in the bible was Job. Why did God choose Job to endure such a great crisis in life? Read Job Chapter 1 and 2 to find out what Job had to endure in life.

_____

_____

_____

_____

_____

Job had seven qualities in Chapter 29 that stood out. Job had a divine continuity with the past (verse 2), he was committed to raising his children (verse 5), he was a man of respect (verse 7), he was a man of mercy (verse 12), he was a man of justice (verse 16), he was a man of stability (verse 19), and he was a man of wisdom (verse 21).

Out of these seven traits, which one do you struggle with the most and why?

_____

_____

_____

_____

_____

Do you think this generation of males has lost their potential to be successful in life? If so, why?

_____

_____

_____

_____

_____

Males are often taught to be hard in life and not show any type of emotions. Do you think this is healthy? Why or why not?

_____

_____

_____

_____

_____

Men often feel like the world has given up on them. What can we do to change this thought process?

_____

_____

_____

_____

What advice would you give to a young man who was struggling to find his way in life?

_____

_____

_____

_____

_____

What is one thing that really helped you in life that you must share with others?

_____

_____

_____

_____

_____

_____

R.A.C.P. MEN

Cooper's Nuggets 4 the week

- ❖ Struggle produces strength!!
- ❖ No one is exempt from going through trials in life.
- ❖ Share your struggles with the generation that is to come.
- ❖ You were born to overcome trials in life.
- ❖ Always remember you are not the only one going through a storm in life.

Question to Consider

❖ What are some positive things that came from a crisis you endured in life?

_____

_____

_____

❖ What are three things you learned from Lesson 6 that you are willing to share with other men?

❖ 1. _____

❖ 2. _____

❖ 3. _____

Point to Ponder

❖ "People aren't attacking you; they're attacking the momentum that God has placed inside of you"- Marquis Cooper

NOTES

LESSON 7

REACHING AND RENEWING MEN

The challenge of the 21st century church is to make the Gospel of Jesus Christ relevant to the needs of men who have lost their way in life. Often when men start off on the wrong track of life, they never find an opportunity to get a fresh start in life. In the 15th Chapter of Luke there is a remarkably familiar parable of the story of the prodigal son. Prodigal means wasteful. The prodigal son in comparison to his older brother made tons of mistakes. The older brother did not make the same mistakes as it relates to wasting his father's money, but the brother had a serious problem with unforgiveness. Unforgiveness is just as deadly as being wasteful. The prodigal son wasted his father's inheritance on riotous (wild) living. He was living his best life until life got very rough for him. All his friends left him because his money ran out, he found himself begging for food, and he ended up in a very dark place in his life. The prodigal son came to a crossroad in his life where he realized he needed to return home to his father's house, but the shame and embarrassment of what he did to his father was a lot for him to deal with. Many of you who are reading this right now may have already dealt with a similar situation in your life or you may know others who lives mirror this story. Many men would have never even thought about returning home especially if they were the one who initiated leaving in the first place.

Let us be honest, most fathers probably would have given that famous speech to the prodigal son, "you made your bed, now lie in it". Most men can probably agree that somewhere in your life you heard someone echo those words to you. The prodigal son's father is not like most men because of the heart he had for his lost son. This father had four unique traits that I will shed light on. The first trait this father had was he was an "approachable father". A man must always be approachable if he plans to teach and reach his child in life. Children should feel safe and comfortable enough to approach you to communicate with you. You will quickly discover that approachable fathers typically have the best relationships with their children and their children's friends. The second trait this father had was he was an "assenting father". The assenting father will sometimes give you what you ask for only to stop you from asking for it again later in life. I have learned in my life that "early frustration eliminates later pain". The assenting father will allow you to hurt a little now, to keep you from dying early (Ecclesiastes 7:17). The third trait this father had was he was an "awaiting father". This is the type of father who will never judge the sins he sees on his child's face, instead he will embrace his potential and fate (his destiny). Sometimes as fathers we must be willing to meet our children at the same place God met us. We can never forget, we were once them. The final trait this father had was he was an "assuring father". An assuring father is the type of father who wants their child(ren) to quickly get back on their feet because they represent you. Most fathers realize the mistakes their children make are the same mistakes they once made.

This final chapter is dedicated to pulling the final pieces together so we can truly R.E.A.C.H. & R.E.N.E.W. for the Kingdom of God. God is the perfect father, but when we follow the plan God has for us; our children will see us as the perfect father.

What are some reasons you think men do not come to church?

_____

_____

_____

_____

_____

Often times men feel alienated and ostracized from the church. What are some things the church needs to do differently to bring men back into the church?

_____

_____

_____

_____

_____

_____

What can you do to support another brother who does not see the need to come to church? What is your duty to help this brother?

_____

_____

_____

_____

_____

_____

The first way we can reach men for the kingdom is to **RESCUE** them by becoming accessible to them. What does this mean?

_____

_____

_____

_____

_____

We must be willing to go where they are geographically. We must meet them where they are. Do you think the church has lost its focus in this area? If so, how do we get the church to understand the importance of this?

_____

_____

_____

_____

_____

_____

The second way we can reach men for the kingdom is to **RESTORE** them by teaching them the foundational principles of life. What happened to the older generation teaching the younger generation?

_____

_____

_____

_____

_____

_____

What are some ways we can redistribute (spread) power to the men in the 21st century? Do most men feel valued in the church? Why or why not?

_____

_____

_____

_____

_____

_____

The third way we can reach men for the kingdom is to **REBUILD** the image of the men within the community. What image do most people have of the man in the 21st century? What can we do to improve the current view?

_____

_____

_____

_____

_____

_____

_____

_____

Read the following image and give your thoughts on how we begin to change this: *A nation of pant SAGGING, interchangeable grill mouth WEARING, bling bling WANTING, big rims SEEKING, foul language USING, sports driven DREAMERS, fashion statement MAKERS, non-vision HAVING, no purpose in life WANTING, silly acting DAILY, non-identity HAVING, name SEEKERS... Can we do anything to change this image in America? How did we get to this point in the first place? Who is responsible for creating this image we now see?*

_____

_____

_____

_____

_____

_____

_____

_____

Romans 5:8 (MSG) reads, *"But God put his love on the line for us by offering his Son in sacrificial death while we were of no use whatever to him"*. What does this scripture teach you about God's love? Do you think you can ever repay God back for the sacrifice he made for you?

_____

_____

_____

_____

_____

_____

Luke 14:23-24 (MSG) reads, *"The master said, 'Then go to the country roads. Whoever you find, drag them in. I want my house full! Let me tell you, not one of those originally invited is going to get so much as a bite at my dinner party."* What did you learn from reading these verses? What does this teach you about Jesus?

_____

_____

_____

_____

_____

_____

The male plays an integral role in its decline and will certainly play a vital role in its incline. What does this mean?

_____

_____

_____

_____

_____

_____

Is there anything wrong with confessing your sins before people? Do you think men feel weak when they must confess their sins openly?

_____

_____

_____

_____

_____

_____

_____

How do we get back to the point of being honest with God?

_____

_____

_____

_____

_____

_____

Why is it so hard for anyone to say they messed up? Is this something you struggle with at times?

_____

_____

_____

_____

_____

_____

We must confess to the Lord what we desire for him to do for us. What does this mean to you?

_____

_____

_____

_____

_____

Philippians 4:6-7(MSG) reads," Don't fret or worry. Instead of worrying, pray. Let petitions and praises shape your worries into prayers, letting God know your concerns. Before you know it, a sense of God's wholeness, everything coming together for good, will come and settle you down. It's wonderful what happens when Christ displaces worry at the center of your life."

What does this scripture teach you about worrying? Which part of the scripture stood out to you the most while you were reading it?

_____

_____

_____

_____

_____

_____

The fourth way we can reach men for the kingdom is to **RELEASE** them from their past. What does this mean? Do you think that people hold on to what you say?

_____

_____

_____

_____

_____

_____

Some men are "drawn to Christ" and others are "driven to Christ". What is the difference between these two phrases? Which category do you see yourself in?

_____

_____

_____

_____

_____

Let us compare Joshua Chapter 2 (Rahab) to Joshua Chapter 7 (Achan)? What lesson is God teaching you in these two chapters? What stood out the most to you as you read these two Chapters of Joshua?

_____

_____

_____

_____

_____

_____

_____

_____

_____

What man played the greatest role in your life spiritually? What separated him from other men?

_____

_____

_____

_____

_____

LESSON 7

REACHING AND RENEWING MEN

Cooper's Nuggets 4 the week

❖ Focus on the Four R's (RESCUE, RESTORE, REBUILD, & RELEASE) daily!!!
❖ Do not isolate yourself from others when you go to church. The enemy always wins in isolation.
❖ Encourage other men to come to church. Use your voice to help win others to Christ.
❖ Be willing to go where the lost men are!!!
❖ Do not allow your past to keep you away from a prosperous future.

Question to Consider

❖ What things in your past, if any, are keeping you from coming back to Christ?

_____

_____

_____

❖ What are three things you learned from Lesson 7 that you are willing to share with other men?

❖ 1. _____

❖ 2. _____

❖ 3. _____

Point to Ponder

❖ "The ultimate measure of a man is not where he stands in moments of comfort and convenience, but where he stands at times of challenge and controversy"- Martin Luther King, Jr.

NOTES

Please take a moment to answer the following questions:

1. What impact has this curriculum had on you? Do you see anything differently in yourself after completing this journey? Are you willing to do anything differently? If so, what changes do you plan to make?

_____

_____

_____

_____

_____

_____

_____

2. How did you see yourself before you started this curriculum compared to how you see yourself now? Have you changed in a major way? If so, how?

_____

_____

_____

_____

_____

_____

_____

3. How do you plan to share what you have learned with other men?

_____

_____

_____

_____

_____

_____

_____

Thank you for taking time to complete this journey with us. At this time, I ask that you provide additional comments on the curriculum you just completed. Please use the space below to share your thoughts as it relates to REACHING and RENEWING men for the kingdom. Please be completely honest because your reflections will help us develop more intriguing curriculums in the future. The evaluation you just completed along with any written comments may be emailed to renewyou@yahoo.com Thank you! It is daytime!!!!

_____

_____

_____

_____

_____

_____

_____

_____

_____

_____

_____

_____

_____

_____

_____

_____

_____

_____

_____

_____

REAL SOLUTIONS 4 REAL MEN

Men's ministry leaders and new member orientation teachers please post this list in various places throughout the church.

1. Give men a voice in the church quickly. If you want to see them, then you must be willing to use them.
2. Plan "get to know you" sessions with all the new men who join your church each quarter. This will help all the new men become acquainted with each other.
3. Partner the new brothers in your church with seasoned brothers (they need role models in the church to help them make a smooth transition).
4. Find out why they left their last church (this is particularly important).
5. Schedule a meeting with all the new men during their first month of joining your church.
6. Have the men who joined your church complete a gift assessment during the first meeting (this will give you or the ministry leader an opportunity to maximize their gift for the Kingdom).
7. Use technology to communicate with them (email, text messages, or Social Media).
8. Do not judge them, let God change them!!!
9. Be supportive, be attentive, and be responsive to help the brothers if needed.
10. See THEM the same way Christ sees YOU!!!

15 TIPS FOR MEN

1. It's OK to be you!
2. Do not hide behind your success!
3. Forgive yourself and keep it moving. Don't let the ability to forgive others hold you hostage.
4. Do not let your ego push you away from God!
5. Always keep your vision in front of you!
6. Surround yourself with positive men who are doing positive things, and getting positive results!
7. Be there for those who need you the most!
8. Always be honest with God about your shortcomings!
9. Don't ever compare your life with the lives of others!
10. Keep pressing until you get to the place God has prepared for you!
11. Don't allow other people to dictate your future!
12. Start decreasing your dependency on other people and learn to tap into your inner gifts!
13. Become more assertive in making your dreams a reality!
14. Don't allow your weakness (the area you need to grow in) to dictate your future!
15. Give back to your community as often as you can!!

MEN WHO ARE MAKING A DIFFERENCE

This section is dedicated to twelve men who are making a difference to bring change to their professions, their families, and their communities. Earlier in your reading I asked you to write about the male who impacted your life the most. This was being asked by me to allow you to reflect on the character traits of that individual. In my life God has allowed me to meet some very influential men. There is no possible way for me to include them all, but I have included twelve who have positively made an impact in my life in some regard. Genesis 4:9- *Then the Lord said to Cain, "Where is your brother Abel?" "I don't know," he replied. "Am I my brother's keeper?"* As men we must all remember God has not called any of us to have a heart like Cain. We should always support, push, encourage, motivate, and stand behind our brothers who are striving to make a difference in this world. In the next few pages you can read about these men who have different backgrounds, different professions, different foundations growing up, but the one consistent thing you will learn about them is each of them have a heat to make a difference. We are our brother's keepers! It is Daytime!!!

AUTOBIOGRAPHIES

Austin Avery III

Gregory Jones

Duane Clayton

Frederick Thrower

Charles Todd

Grover Garrison

Don Lemon Jr.

Corey Foreman

David Whitaker

Carl Smith

Raymond Brock

Ralph Nelson

AUSTIN AVERY III -

Fish-N-Loaves - Executive Director

Austin Avery III is a son of The Most High God, husband of Laresia Avery, and dad of Josiah Avery.

As Executive Director, and co-founder of Fish-N-Loaves, Austin's primary role is to provide vision and direction for the organization as it relates to its sustainability and social services initiatives. He also:

—Collaborates with government officials and food practitioners on ways to improve food access in the Mid-South and beyond including design and implementation strategies with a primary focus being placed on access-controlled bread boxes, semi-automated Aquaponics community gardens and the associated Hungernomics.org centralized partner management web portal.

—Spearheads the organization's distribution efforts including its solar-powered "Meals on Wheels" bus (in the past) and other delivery vehicles which delivers meals and excess food to the residents of Hernando, MS x Nesbit, MS x Eudora, MS x Frayser, TN x Millington, TN, North Memphis, TN, the CBU Food Recovery Network, Olive Branch, MS and Southaven, MS (starting March 2018), etc.

—Coordinates periodic "Life Touch" Community Outreach events in which he serves poverty-stricken, crime-ridden, inner city communities in Tennessee such as Frayser, North Memphis, East Memphis, Whitehaven, Munford, and Atoka where the primary purpose is to provide hope and tangible solutions to overcoming economic and literacy barriers.

—Co-facilitates an ad-hoc business incubator to assist aspiring entrepreneurs from the inner city with writing business plans including calculation of startup costs, analysis of break-even metrics, establishment of go-live dates and other pertinent milestones as well as training the entrepreneurs on basic bookkeeping practices.

—Serves as an advocate and mentor, periodically, in Mid-South high schools and community centers aimed at equipping youth with the tools needed to understand individual responsibility to neighbors and community.

For more details, please visit http://fish-n-loaves.org or https://hungernomics.org.

GREGORY JONES

Assistant Principal, North Little Rock Middle School

Gregory Jones is an Administrator in the North Little Rock School District. Currently, he is the Assistant Principal at North Little Rock Middle School in North Little Rock, Arkansas. While at NLRMS, he partners with the building principal to provide a safe and nurturing environment for all students, where intellectual, emotional, social, and physical needs are met and expanded into lifelong learning skills.

After spending over 20 years in education, Gregory views *a collaborative school environment as the key to creating successful teachers and students. He believes partnerships with parents and communities are essential to enriching the experience at North Little Rock Middle School.* Gregory says, *"it is my goal to know each student by name and by need",* it is how well you connect with the students you're trying to communicate with".

Before becoming an Administrator, Gregory taught 1st, 2nd, and 5th grade students. He also worked for the Arkansas Department of Education as a Standards Assurance Specialist. In 2015, he completed The Arkansas Leadership Academy – Assistant Principal Institute. Gregory holds a bachelor's degree in Elementary Education from The University of Arkansas at Pine Bluff. He also received his master's degree and Educational Specialist Degree in Education Administration from UA Little Rock.

DUANE CLAYTON

Principal, Mills High School

Duane is a product of the Magnolia Public Schools where he credits Merilyn Schambach and many others for planting valuable seeds. Duane, an Honor Graduate at Magnolia High School, attended Southern Arkansas University on a minority teachers' scholarship while spending a brief two years on the Mulerider Football Team. Clayton recalls the lesson of his administrators: Terry Bo Ray and Jim Garrett in Fellowship of Christian Athletes.

Clayton graduated from SAU with a Bachelor of Science in Art Education in 1999. He immediately began his teaching career in Springhill, LA. He married MarKa' Scott-Clayton, his high school sweetheart in 2000. MarKa' is a utilization review coordinator at the Bridgeway Hospital in North Little Rock, AR. Clayton has two children Marnaya Cook (24 yrs. old 2014 Arkansas State Graduate) and Makala Clayton (19 yrs. old Mills University Studies High graduate and current sophomore at UALR). Mr. Clayton has two grandchildren Bell (5 months and Jacobi Cook, Jr. 3 years)

Duane gave in to follow Christ with his complete being in 2006 and later surrendered to the call to minister. In 2007, Minister Duane Clayton preached his first sermon and was licensed to preach the gospel of Jesus Christ. In December 2007, Clayton completed his master's degree in educational leadership. Since this time, Clayton has served as a teacher, ministry leader, assistant principal, coach, father, husband, Pulaski County Jail religious volunteer, and most of all servant of God. 3 years ago, Duane began taking up a running as a hobby. He completed over 30 marathons and half marathons.

Clayton is serving in a new capacity as the building principal of the 610 student Mills University Studies High School in Little Rock where God has planted him. Clayton does not want to be popular, but effective. "To God be the Glory for the Things He has done." This summer Clayton will be the closing speaker for the school improvement conference.

FREDERICK THROWER

Founder of YBL (Young Brothers Leading)

Frederick Tremayne Thrower was born in Las Vegas, Nevada but raised in Fordyce, Arkansas. He graduated from Fordyce High School with honors and then moved to Fayetteville, Arkansas to major in Industrial Engineering at the University of Arkansas. While at the U of A, Frederick was active in many organizations such as Blue Key Honor Society, Order of Omega, and Who's Who Among Students in American Universities and Colleges, and served as president of the Kappa Kappa Chapter of Alpha Phi Alpha Fraternity, Incorporated. Upon completion of an internship following his junior year, Frederick decided he wanted to become a teacher. He earned a Bachelor of Arts in Mathematical Sciences and a Master of Arts in Teaching.

Frederick started his career in secondary education as a math teacher at Northside High School in Fort Smith, Arkansas. He also served as an adjunct professor at the University of Arkansas at Fort Smith. Frederick has served on the Partners in Education Committee, the Principal's Focus Team, the Fort Smith Classroom Teachers Association, and the African American Heritage Committee during his tenure at Northside High School.

One of his proudest achievements since he started teaching was founding a new student organization called Young Brothers Leading (**YBL**). The purpose of YBL is to develop leaders who promote brotherhood and academic excellence while serving their school and community with ambition, integrity, and responsibility. The goals of YBL are to instill values that will help young men succeed in school and life, improve academic performance, identify career goals, develop familiarity with colleges and college resources, and participate in mentoring with local professionals. The diverse group of young men who have joined YBL have volunteered for the Gospel Rescue Mission, Project Compassion, the Fort Smith Community Clearinghouse, and the Arkansas Dream Center.

Frederick is married to the love of his life, Lynette Wright Thrower. They attend church at the House of Restoration where they both serve on the praise and worship team and work in the children's church.

CHARLES TODD

Career Transition Specialist

Charles Todd is a 1987 Graduate of Parkview High School. Charles served five years in the U.S. Marine Corp. Todd presently serves as the Career Transition Specialist with Arkansas Juvenile Assessment and Treatment Center. Todd is a 1997 Graduate of Remington College with an Associate Degree in Medical Assisting, a 2004 Graduate of Samuel Merritt University with Bachelor of Science in Health & Human Sciences, and a 2010 Graduate of University of Phoenix with Master of Business Administration.

Todd is a Member of Omega Psi Phi Fraternity, Inc. He is the Chairman of the Omega Prostate/Colon Cancer Awareness 5K Run/Walk. He has chaired this event for the past five years which has allowed him the opportunity to serve as the Volunteer Community Health Advisor with the American Cancer Society. Charles is a 3 Time Basileus Award Winner of Pi Omicron Chapter of Omega Psi Phi Fraternity, Inc, and an Unsung Hero Award Winner of Pi Omicron Chapter of Omega Psi Phi Fraternity, Inc.

GROVER GARRISON

Educator/Coach

Grover Garrison is a Pre AP-World History Teacher at Sylvan Hills High School in the Pulaski County Special School District. Garrison also serves as the 9th Grade Boys Head Basketball Coach and the Girls Head Track and Field Coach at Sylvan Hills High School. Grover attained his Associates Degree in Psychology from Eastern (OK) State College, his B.A. Degree in Psychology from Texas Southern University, and presently is pursuing his Education Administration Certification from UA Little Rock.

Grover was selected as a U.S. Emerging Elite Coach (50 per year Nationwide), USATF Level 2 Certified Coach, and USTFCCAA Certified Coach. Grover has attained 1 State Championship, 5 Conference Championships, 41 Conference Champions, 12 Individual Event State Champions, and 5x Track Conference Coach of the Year.

Grover says, "he wants all of his students both on and off the court to reach their maximum potential in life. It is my goal to always connect with my students to let them know that hard work does pay off if you don't quit".

DON LEE LEMONS JR.

SAU Tech Rockets head junior varsity coach

Donald Lee Lemons Jr. is a 2004 graduate of Hall High school. In addition to being a graduate of Hall, he also prides himself in the fact that he is a graduate of the P.A.R.K. (Positive Atmosphere Reaches Kids) program. This program was founded by former NFL player Keith Jackson in 1989. Keith Jackson had a vision to help teenagers overcome the obstacles of violence and troubled lives. This is where I learned the true meaning of the word leadership, and what being a mentor truly looked like.

In life I live by the motto, "I am my brother's keeper". This simply means no matter what obstacles I may face in my personal life; I must strive to help the next person overcome the trials and tribulations they face in life. This is what was taught and embedded into me for years and years, and now this is what I must teach and share with the next generation.

Don recently accepted a new position as the head junior varsity coach at SAU Tech. Don also coaches AAU basketball in Little Rock, Arkansas. He has been coaching off and on for the past five years. He coaches a 5th grade team of young men, and a team of high school boys. The thrill and joy of seeing these young men grow into productive men is the reason he does what he does. Most of them just need to know that someone believes in them and wants them to succeed in life. I genuinely enjoy it. I just hope and pray that the young men I work with can pass on the knowledge, wisdom, and teachings to the next generation. This is what being "my brother's keeper is all about". We must reach back and help those who need our help.

COREY FOREMAN

Case Worker Kids for the Future, Inc.

Elder Corey Foreman is a humble and native servant of Lee County, Arkansas. An avid evangelist who has been anointed to work for God, Elder Foreman joined the staff of Kingdom Connections Church in 2005 and became an ordained Associate Minister of the Gospel of Jesus Christ two years later. He currently serves as Youth Minister, a position he has held for the past fifteen years. In this capacity, he gives vision and leadership to the church's most sacred members—its youth. In 2007, Elder Foreman founded Boys II Men, a youth development program that aims to provide tools for youth to explore, expand, and build their faith through education, encouragement, and support. He often times proclaims to the youth that ". . . where you are today is *not* really where you are; but when you have faith, you can go places, and when you get there, you can do things."

In addition to fulfilling his ministerial duties at Kingdom Connections, Elder Foreman bares the responsibilities associated with being a case worker, advisor, and student. He works as a case worker for Kids for the Future, Inc. where he addresses the mental health needs of children and young adults. He is also an active member of the Our Story Conference and the Writing for the Soul Workshop Boards of Directors. Corey is also on the Board of Directors for Court Appointed Special Advocates (CASA) of Arkansas Delta for foster children.

Elder Foreman holds a Bachelor of Arts in Business Administration Degree as well as Bachelor and master's degrees in Christian Counseling. Corey recently graduated with his second masters from Amridge University where he is received a Master of Arts in Professional Counseling. In his spare time, he can be found traveling, reading, cooking, meeting new people, planning events, and living up to his motto, *"I just want to be into what God is up to."*

DAVID JR WHITAKER

Red Sea Cooking & Catering

Growing up on the East Coast, it was at the age of 13 when David realized he had a passion for cooking. By the age of 16, he had mastered many dishes, but still had a long way to go. It was in his 20s when he started working in different restaurants to strengthen his skills. Things were not always the best growing up, but he was determined to overcome the obstacles of life. One day while having a seizure, Jay heard God speak to him, and from that day forward, it has been his purpose to share the word of God with everyone he meets. His passion for cooking led him to start Red Sea Cooking & Catering in 2017.

Red Sea Cooking & Catering received its name from studying the word of God and remembering how Moses freed the people from Egypt. As they were going through the Red Sea, they had to keep the faith and continue trusting in God to push forward. Chef Jay's plan is to keep trusting God and keep bringing the best of the best from Red Sea Cooking & Catering.

Website: https://redseacookingcater.wixsite.com/redsea
Facebook: Red Sea Cooking
Instagram: redseacooking.catering
Phone:646-675-5973
Email: redseacooking.catering@gmail.com

CARL SMITH

CEO God's Children on The Move

Carl Smith is the CEO/Founder of the Non-Profit God's Children on The Move. Carl was born in North Little Rock, Arkansas (Dixie Addition) to a family of nine. Carl graduated from Northeast High School in 1987. He began his work career with the Sanitation/Solid Waste department in North Little Rock when he was 20 years old. By the time he turned 23, he was appointed as the Supervisor over the Solid Waste Department. Carl completed his education and received his bachelor's degree in Criminal Justice in 2007. During that time, he also started a successful company cleaning floors where that he managed for 13 years. Carl currently works for Union Pacific Railroad (Koppers, ink). His true passion is to help the youth of his community to reach their God given potential in life. Carl is Married to Tonya Smith and they have 5 children and 8 grandchildren.

Contact information: 501.551.6956
Website: www.godschildrenonthemove.com
Email address: GCOTM2020@gmail.com

RAYMOND BROCK

Inspirational Speaker/Life Coach

Raymond Brock is an inspirational Speaker and Life Coach from Little Rock, Arkansas, where he founded Humble Living, LLC in 2017. He is passionate about teaching others the peace and love of God. He loves to share about his own personal relationship and walk with Christ so that others can know and experience a life of Humility, Gratefulness, Confidence, and Peace.

Over the past two years, as a(n):

Inspirational Speaker- Mr. Brock has been empowering youth in grades K-12 on different topics such as self -branding, handling responsibilities at home, the importance of obedience, taking initiative and more.

Life Coach- Mr. Brock has consulted with both men and women on parenting, improving relationships, the importance of integrity, and building a relationship with God, being a positive role model, and branding their marriage.

Community Outreach Advocate- While Mr. Brock has volunteered and interacted with the homeless population and other community projects, his current focus, however, is showing love and compassion for the community youth. He does this through free, interactive children events that also include a teaching/training collaboration on life and basketball skills.

For booking Info, Contact Raymond Brock at: 501.541.6913
Website: www.humbleliving.org
Email address: humbleliving123@gmail.com

RALPH NELSON

Captain, Little Rock Fire Department, Little Rock, Arkansas

Ralph is the oldest son of Ralph and Maude Nelson with one sibling brother Reggie L. Nelson and the father to one teenage daughter Grayce Allison Nelson.

Ralph Leon Nelson was born October 14th, 1968 in Arkadelphia Arkansas. He grew up on his grandparent's farm on highway 26 just west of Arkadelphia. His education started at Central Elementary school in Arkadelphia before moving to Alexander, Arkansas and attending Bryant Elementary, Middle, Junior High and then graduating from Bryant High in 1987. He was elected as the first African American Senior Class President in Bryant High School history. He then went on to attend Phillips County Community College in Helena, Arkansas in 1987-88.

He entered the United States Marine Corps in May of 1988 and served in the Marine Reserves until 1994. His MOS or military job was a diesel mechanic/vehicle recovery. He served in the one conflict Desert Shield/Storm in 1990-1991. He received numerus awards, while he was in the Marine Corps. Those awards include National Defense Service Medal; Southwest Asia Service Medal; Kuwait Liberation Medal; Sea Service Deployment Ribbon; Navy USCG Unit Commendation Ribbon and the Meritorious Unit Commendation Ribbon and he is also a Marine Corps veteran.

After his military enlistment and some mediocre jobs and through a blessing from a church find, he was able to apply and become a professional fire fighter for the city of Little Rock, Arkansas in 1995. He has diligently worked hard in his training and knowledge of his craft and was promoted to Engineer (Driver) in 2001 and then promoted to the rank of Captain in 2014. He has served as chairman of the LRFD Peer Group; a member of the Arkansas Crisis Team and now is a member of ARLEAP (Arkansas Law Enforcement Assistance Program. Those organization all assist people who are in crisis or having mental or emotional issues due to severe trauma incidents, job conflicts or family and marital problems.

He has had several struggles in his life that involved him not being able to completely fit in with any one category. Always having to prove that he could be just as good as others in any endeavor that he chose to pursue. He considered himself a bit of an eccentric person who likes many different genres of music and can relate with many different types of people. He was taught at an early age to never look down upon or judge anyone. Racial discrimination has also been quite a struggle in his life. Caucasian verses African American. Being African American made it hard to be accepted by Caucasian's and in the eyes of African American's, he was not black enough.

He turned to sports to be that equalizer to bridge the gap and be accepted by everyone. Working hard to be one of the best in each sport that he played. He participated in many different sports growing up, baseball; track; football and basketball. He became good enough to earn a basketball scholarship and played 1987-88 year of basketball at Phillips County Community College.

His family and extended family was a legacy filled with deep family connections and strong spiritual values. He was always searching and trying to find his purpose in life. Following in the footsteps of his father who was always involved in church, he took that which his father had installed in him and pushed it to a higher level and become an Ordained Deacon in 2005 and then an Ordained Minister in 2015.

Life is starting to make sense now, and everything that happened and went on in his life is slowly staring to all merge together. Trusting his faith and not leaning on his own understanding, but allowing God to lead him has molded him into the person he is today.

Attending a high school that made him aware of the color of his skin pushed him to hold steady and become stronger mentally to get through. He is a true believer in everything happens for a reason. Romans 8:28 is very evident in his life because of everything he has been through. He is now able to use the skills he learned to help other's which is God's mission for his life. He hopes to continue to be able to listen and hear God and be more effective as a man, father, son, brother, family member, Minister, co-worker, and friend. Ralph presently serves as an Associate Minister & the Ministry Coordinator/Director at Otter Creek Community Church in Little Rock, Arkansas.

COOPER'S NUGGETS 4 LIFE

"Just because you're surrounded by folks doesn't mean you are surrounded by followers."- Marquis L. Cooper

"True arrival is the ability to deposit into someone else. If you're not helping others your journey hasn't even started yet."- Marquis L. Cooper

"Doubt and fear from your past can derail you from being successful in your future."- Marquis L. Cooper

"Stop going overboard to please people who don't even like you. Put that energy into something else."- Marquis L. Cooper

"People don't hate you; they just hate the fact that they can't stop what's in you."- Marquis L. Cooper

"Sometimes in life you have to remove yourself, (get rid of distractions) so you can see yourself."- Marquis L. Cooper

"If you leave and grow, you can come back and plant."- Marquis L. Cooper

"The past holds the key to the present, and the present holds access to the future."- Marquis L. Cooper

"When the man is out of place, the woman becomes displaced, and the children become misplaced."- Marquis L. Cooper

"When your present is not in order, your future is in danger of being chaotic."- Marquis L. Cooper

"A secure leader will put you out front, a scared leader will put you behind, and an insecure leader will put you out."- Marquis L. Cooper

"The quieter it gets, the closer you are. Learn how to trust the silence." - Marquis L. Cooper

AUTHOR'S CORNER

Marquis is the Senior Pastor of Otter Creek Community Church in Little Rock, Ar. He is a 1994 graduate of Lee High School in Marianna, AR. He obtained the following degrees: A Bachelor of Arts degree from Philander Smith College, and a master's degree in Counseling Education from the University of Arkansas at Little Rock. While attending Philander Smith College he was a recipient of the Walton Delta Scholarship. He recently had the opportunity to take part in an Oral History project through the Walton Foundation. He is a licensed counselor for grades K-12 in the states of Arkansas and Tennessee.

Mr. Cooper was appointed to serve on the Suicide Prevention Council which was the first of its kind for Arkansas. Mr. Cooper has received many honors over the past few years. Some of which include: the JV Educational Leadership Award, Citizen of the Year Award, Moton Strong-Lee Hall of Fame Inductee, Character Education Partnership as a National Promising Practice in Washington, D.C., and the SRS Community Leader of the Year.

Cooper is an accomplished educator. He has presented for multiple associations which include; National Center for Youth Issues, TCA (Tennessee Counseling Association), APCA (Arkansas

Parent Coordinators Association), ArSCA (Arkansas School Counseling Association), AEA (Arkansas Education Association), TCA (Texas Counseling Association), and the Multicultural Counseling Association. He offers professional development workshops to educators across the state of Arkansas, and since 2009, he has presented his workshop to thousands of educators, parents, and students on behalf of the AEA Association.

Cooper wrote and published *Guidance -N- Action* in 2008. In 2010, he published *Sista Let Me Tell Ya, Bruh If You Only Knew*. In 2012, he published R.E.N.E.W. (Removing Every Negative Emotion & Word). R.E.N.E.W. is a curriculum designed for students ages 13 and up. In 2014, Cooper was featured in a book entitled "A Matter of Life or Death: Why Black Men must save black boys in public education".

He and his wife Karmen have three children and presently reside in Little Rock, AR

CONTACT INFORMATION

To Book Marquis Cooper for the following adult or youth related events, please send an email to renewyou@yahoo.com or call 901-786-2322

Educational Professional Development Workshops

1. Title- Guidance- N- Action
   - **Summary:** This workshop will provide information to educators on ways to maximize student leadership beginning with students in the first grade.

   - **Target Grade Level and Subject:** Elementary and Middle school counselors, first year school counselors, administrators, curriculum specialists, and teachers

   - **Length of session:** 2, 4, or 6-hour session

   - **Workshop qualifications**- Cooper has presented for multiple associations which include; National Center for Youth Issues, TCA (Tennessee Counseling Association), APCA (Arkansas Parent Coordinators Association), ArSCA (Arkansas School Counseling Association), AEA (Arkansas Education Association), TCA (Texas Counseling Association), AR Safe Schools Association, Multicultural Counseling Association, and the High School Principals Institute in Memphis, Tn. He offers professional development workshops to educators across the state of Arkansas, and since 2009, he has presented his workshop to thousands of educators, parents, and students on behalf of the AEA Association.

2. Title- 25 Tips to A Successful School Year
   - **Summary:** This workshop will offer effective strategies to help teachers eliminate unknown biases when working with students.

   - **Target Grade Level and Subject:** Elementary, Middle, and Secondary educators, ALC/ALE staff members, school counselors, administrators, and mental health providers

   - **Length of session:** 2-hour session

3. Title- R.E.N.E.W. (Removing Every Negative Emotion & Word)
   - **Summary:** This workshop will provide effective strategies to maximize student leadership, improve grades, decrease retention rates, and help close the communication gap between students, teachers, and parents.
   - **Target Grade Level and Subject:** Middle and high school counselors, first year school counselors, teachers, PLC team leaders, school administrators, parent liaisons, and curriculum specialist
   - **Length of session:** 2, 4, or 6-hour session

4. Title- MISSING: Find OUR children. OUR selves. OUR hope.
   - **Summary:** This workshop will provide strategies on how to effectively combat social media pressures, personal/ social issues, gang involvement, and educational distractions. This workshop will also shed light on the four goals of misbehavior.
   - **Target Grade Level and Subject:** Parents, Elementary, middle, and high school counselors, teachers, PTA members, administrators, and paraprofessionals
   - **Length of session:** 2-hour session

5. It Takes A Village: Youth Leaders Workshop
   - **Summary:** This workshop will teach youth leaders how to build relationships with youth, how to encourage positive healthy behavior in youth, and how to get parents more involved with youth related activities.
   - **Target Audience:** Youth facility directors, daycare owners, community organizations, church leaders, after school program coordinators, teachers, counselors, etc.…
   - **Length of session:** 2, 4, or 6-hour session

6. Title: Battling the Barriers of Education
   - **Summary of Workshop:** To build and strengthen relationships among faculty and staff, teachers, and students. This workshop will also focus on team building activities, communication skills, building positive relationships, enhancing cultural differences, and creating a shared vision among all stakeholders.
   - **Targeted Grade Level and Subject:** Secondary teachers, paraprofessionals, instructional facilitators, PTA members, school counselors, school social workers, teachers, and building level administrators
   - **Length of session:** 6-hour session (1- or 2-day workshop)

Keynote Speaking:
Marquis is a highly requested nationally renowned motivational keynote speaker for conferences, summits, banquets, family reunions, and educational conferences. He is a former presenter for the National Center for Youth Issues. His presence is highly regarded because of his personalized unique approach of gaining audience participation. His style is unique, infectious, alive, thought

provoking, engaging, humorous, and moving. He possesses a gift that captivates the attention of all his audience members.

"The progression of his presentation is inspiring and is the most compelling presentation I've ever attended since becoming a teacher in 1991."- **Dianna Harshfield, M. Ed., J.A. Fair High School of College and Career Academies**

*"His presentation is amazing. Every educator, administrator, and parent need to hear him."-***Mandy Smith, Newport Elementary School 4th grade teacher**

"This is a powerful message that everyone needs to hear."- **Vanessa Carter, Upward Bound Youth Coordinator, UAPB**

"The session was educational, entertaining, and thought provoking. It was one of the best workshops I've ever attended."- **Frederick Thrower, North Side High School Educator**

Church Services:

As an ordained minister, Pastor Marquis Cooper speaks at church events for men, women, youth, singles, as well as family events. Sought after for his unique unorthodox style, he delivers anointed life changing messages that leave people with inspiration and hope.

Women's Ministry:

Pastor Cooper delivers anointed messages at retreats, workshops, and special events that address women's issues in a unique way that yields a renewal of spirit. He has a unique gift that empowers women to discover their true purpose in life.

Men's Ministry:

Pastor Cooper delivers anointed, interactive keynotes, retreats, workshops, and special events that address men's issues in a way which allows them to heal. He has a unique gift that empowers men to tap into the gifts they have been given.

Youth Assemblies:

Mr. Cooper partners with elementary, middle, and high schools to provide thought provoking and high energy grade level assemblies. He speaks to thousands of students each year. He offers school level assemblies on motivation, leadership, relationships, and healthy living. He can develop workshops based on the needs of the school or organization.

Educational Consulting:

Mr. Cooper provides educational consulting to school districts, as well as providing professional development trainings and motivational workshops to inspire, motivate, and reignite educators and staff members. His events for educators renew them in every aspect imaginable.

"Mr. Cooper was straight-forward, honest, and passionate in the delivery of his presentation. He involved the audience, including the children, making each one feel valued. He was not a stranger and each participant, regardless of age, gender, and race seemed to have been positively affected by Mr. Cooper. The evaluations of the conference revealed that the participants wanted one thing more than anything else—more of Mr. Cooper" - **Mary Hayden, Principal Anna Strong Learning Academy- Lee County School District**

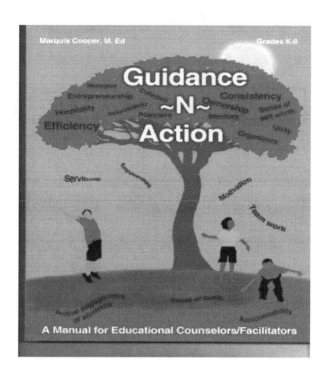

Guidance ~N~ Action is preparation endowed with an infinite affiliation for success. This curriculum was written for school counselors who work with students' grades K-8. This program is designed to cultivate the traditional stance of public-school life to an elevated advancement that involves closing the gap between the children that are "celebrated" and those that are "tolerated". Children often steer where they stare, however with proper guidance imparted they can be groomed into being responsible, well rounded adults. Moreover, the vision entails the conception of liberation for every child to push past their immediate environment to reach the climax of possibilities for tomorrow. The program is patterned to transform dreams into reality with the energetic concept of GGL (**G**o expecting, **get** what you came for, and **L**eave Smiling). Guidance ~N~ Action was recognized as a model program on the National Dropout Prevention website in late 2010.

Purchase at www.authorhouse.com

SISTA LET
ME TELL YA,
BRUH IF YOU
ONLY KNEW

*Real Talk for Parents and Educators,
From Me to You*

MARQUIS COOPER

The words are so profound and timely and relevant to people of ALL ages and backgrounds. The flow of the book is spot on. The opening chapter sets an enthralling tone for the rest of the book. It reminds us "Ignorance is NOT bliss, it's simply Ignorance". I cannot imagine families NOT reading this book together. It is a MUST read for book clubs, youth groups, parents, pastors, educators, etc. The book has a vernacular that is REAL and easy to understand on all levels. This message will change and enlighten the lives of both students and educators, and hopefully will reverse some of the unique challenges that African American students are faced with throughout the nation. The book was not just written for African Americans, but was written with all ethnicities in mind.

Purchase at www.authorhouse.com

The R.E.N.E.W. curriculum sheds light on the past, while opening the lines of communication in the present. This curriculum will help shift the vicious cycle of negativity which occurs in communities, homes, and schools every day. By utilizing this curriculum, students will fully be able to recognize & break down the "how and why" of their current situation. This will in turn lead students to greater academic, personal/social, and career opportunities in life.

Students will gain a clearer perspective on how to repair the issues they are dealing with in life. The curriculum provides practical advice on how to identify, approach, and move toward solutions to help close the communication gap which currently plagues many students, parents, and educators within our society in the 21st century.

This 136-page curriculum is designed for students in grades 7-12 who attend public, private, or charter schools. The curriculum can be used with all students, but the curriculum has made a tremendous difference with at-risk youth, ALE students, juvenile detention students, or any students who are in jeopardy of being retained. The curriculum is also designed for college freshmen. The curriculum has various chapters to help empower students, parents, and educators.

Purchase at www.authorhouse.com

ENDNOTES

1. https://datacenter.kidscount.org/data/tables/107-children-in-single-parent-families-by-race#detailed/1/any/false/37,871,870,573,869,36,868,867,133,38/9,12,1,13/432,431
2. https://www.fatherhood.org/father-absence-statistic
3. https://www.pewresearch.org/fact-tank/2020/05/06/black-imprisonment-rate-in-the-u-s-has-fallen-by-a-third-since-2006/
4. https://www.pewtrusts.org/en/research-and-analysis/articles/2018/12/06/community-supervision-marked-by-racial-and-gender-disparities
5. https://news.umich.edu/police-sixth-leading-cause-of-death-for-young-black-men/
6. https://nces.ed.gov/programs/raceindicators/indicator_rda.asp
7. https://www.thenation.com/article/archive/by-2030-one-in-three-us-prisoners-will-be-over-50/

Printed in the United States
by Baker & Taylor Publisher Services